We were there

THE

1950s

Rosemary Rees

Heinemann

Heinemann Library,
an imprint of Heinemann Publishers (Oxford) Ltd,
Halley Court, Jordan Hill, Oxford, OX2 8EJ

OXFORD LONDON EDINBURGH
MADRID PARIS ATHENS BOLOGNA
MELBOURNE SYDNEY AUCKLAND
SINGAPORE TOKYO IBADAN
NAIROBI GABORONE HARARE
PORTSMOUTH NH (USA)

First published 1993
93 94 95 96 10 9 8 7 6 5 4 3 2 1

British Library Cataloguing in Publication Data
is available on request from the British Library.

ISBN 0 431 07327 9

Designed by Philip Parkhouse
Printed and bound in China

Acknowledgements
The author and publisher would like to thank the following
for permission to reproduce photographs:
Advertising Archive: p. 21
Hulton Picture Company: pp. 7, 8, 12, 13, 15, 16, 17, 23, 26, 28, 29
Robert Opie Collection: p. 18
Popperfoto: pp. 6, 19, 20, 25, 27
Con Dawson: pp. 22, 24, 30
Topham: pp. 4, 5, 9, 10, 11, 14

Cover photograph: Hulton Picture Company

The author and publisher would like to thank all of the people who
contributed memories for this book.

Note to the reader
In this book there are some words in the text
which are printed in **bold type**. This shows that
the words are listed in the glossary on page 31.
The glossary gives a brief explanation of words
that may be new to you.

Contents

Home 1

A lot of new houses and some new towns were built in the 1950s. These houses were built in Corby new town, in Northamptonshire.

Fiona Gray remembers her childhood in Essex.

I remember moving to our brand new house. Even though it was new, it was still always cold at home. I hated getting out of bed in a cold room with frost on the inside of the windows to get dressed for school.

I had plenty of layers to put on. First, was a woolly vest. On top of that was a liberty bodice. This was a white cotton waistcoat lined with soft cotton fleece. The buttons were rubber, so they would not crack when they were washed. I wore two pairs of knickers: white ones as linings, and navy blue baggy ones over them. Next I put on my white woollen school blouse, my tie, gymslip and cardigan. I wore brown socks up to my knees, and brown lace-up shoes.

I had a navy blue waterproof coat, a navy blue **velour** hat and a scarf. I must have looked like Humpty Dumpty with pig-tails! In spite of all this, I was never really warm.

Sue Mann remembers moving to a new house

Until I was 3-years-old, we lived in a flat in Islington. Then we moved to a new house in Swindon. We had much more space – and a bathroom! We had new 'G-Plan' furniture: red tub chairs and a settee, which converted into a bed for visitors; a light wood dining table and chairs with red **leatherette** seats, and a sideboard with glass sliding doors. We also had our first fridge, and a **radiogram.**

Derek Patterson remembers bathtime when he was a boy.

We got our first bath in 1957. There was no room for it upstairs, so it went in the kitchen. It had a lid on it so that it could be used as a worktop when no one was bathing. We were allowed to have a bath once a week. The lid had a latch on it to keep it shut. My older brother would often put the lid down and the latch on when I was in the bath. I had to kick and shout to get my Mum to let me out.

This was part of an advert. It shows a family and the inside of their house in the 1950s.

Home 2

The boy and girl in this picture were celebrating the end of sweet rationing after the war.

Geoff Lancaster remembers the end of rationing.

I was born in 1938, and so I had never known what it was like to be able to go into a shop and buy what I wanted without a **ration book**. The shop keeper always cut coupons out of the book for the food that was rationed. It was really strange to be told to throw away our ration books. From 1953, we could buy anything we liked in the shops as long as we had the money. It took a lot of getting used to.

Janet Withersby remembers the end of sweet rationing.

Until I was 9-years-old sweets were rationed. Sweet rationing ended just before Coronation Day, in 1953. It was a very special day for all children. Many children from my school had a **threepenny bit** to spend at the sweetshop on the way home. This was so that they could celebrate the wonderful day. For weeks and weeks we spent all our pocket money on sweets and ice creams.

Margaret Simpkins remembers what her mother did each week.

My mother and my grandmother had a routine. On Mondays they washed the clothes, and on Tuesdays they **starched**, ironed and aired them on the wooden clothes horse that stood in front of the fire for days.

Wednesdays was 'upstairs', and the beds and dressing tables would be moved and cleaned under, as well as being dusted and polished. On Thursdays the rooms downstairs were cleaned, and the outside yard scrubbed clean. In the evening the dried fruit for the weekend baking was put to soak. My gran baked slabs of loaf cake every weekend.

On Fridays my Mum went shopping for the weekend. She usually went to our local **Co-op**. On Saturday afternoons we always went by bus to the market. Every Sunday we had a full roast dinner at mid-day. Most Sundays my aunts and cousins came round in the afternoon for a high tea.

This family are having their tea. They all lived in a town in Lancashire. Most of the adults worked in a cotton mill.

Home 3

This woman lived on Tyneside in the north-east of England. She has found a good place to hang out her family washing!

Janet Withersby remembers her mother's new washing machine.
In 1951 my mother and father went to London to visit the **Festival of Britain.** There, my mother saw the new electric washing machines. When she got home to Liverpool, she complained and complained about washday until she got one of the new machines.

My mother thought her new machine would do all the washing for her, but it was not at all like the washing machines of today. She had to fill it with hot water from the sink, and when the washing was finished, use a small hose pipe to empty the water out and down the sink. Inside the washing machine was a sort of paddle that was powered by electricity. It went round and round and swooshed the clothes and soapy water about. There was a **mangle** at the back of the washing machine, to squeeze water out of the clothes. The rollers were powered by electricity. You had to be very careful not to get your fingers squashed!

This was one of the very first launderettes. People who didn't have a washing machine at home could come here and pay to use one.

Joan Hudson remembers going to the launderette when it first opened in Sheppey, in Kent.
When you went to the launderette, you could choose whether to do the washing yourself, or to leave it and have it done by someone who worked there. Most people did their own washing, because you had to pay more to have it done. The washing was almost always done by women. Women who went out to work often left their washing to be done for them.

You used two machines, a washer and a spin drier. The spin drier didn't get the clothes very dry so you always took wet clothes home.

We called it the 'Bendix', not the launderette, because Bendix was the name on all the machines. It was very busy, and you often had to wait until it was your turn to use one of the machines.

You took your own washing powder or bought a cupful from the person in charge.

School 1

This school was built in London, in 1954.

Rosemary Dawson remembers the first school she went to.

The one thing I really wanted to do was to be milk monitor. The milkman delivered crates of little bottles of milk every morning. The milk monitor's job was to make a hole in every silver bottle top with a **skewer**, and push a paper straw through into the milk. After playtime, when everyone had finished their milk, the milk monitor threw the straws away and washed the bottles and the silver tops very carefully. He (or she) put the clean bottles back in the crate for the milkman to collect, and put the clean silver foil tops into a special box. When we had saved enough, we were going to buy a guide dog for a blind person with them.

I was never chosen to be milk monitor. A boy called Jeremy Killinger usually got the job. I always had to put away the **raffia** after craft lessons, which was not nearly as important as being milk monitor.

Margaret Simpkins remembers playtimes at her primary school in Wales.

We played different games at different times of the year. In the spring we played **whip and top**. The whips were brightly coloured and the **thongs** were leather, but we replaced them with cord because they worked better. The tops were pale wood, with red and blue stripes. After a while we chalked patterns on them in bright colours. It was as much fun to chalk the patterns as to see them spinning in bright colours. In the summer we skipped, turning a long heavy rope and chanting "All in together girls..." as we all tried to jump the rope as it turned. We played hopscotch, too.

In the autumn, we played marbles with the boys. All of the other games the girls played by themselves. In winter, in the underground shelter, we played 'Farmer's in his den', 'In and out the bonnie bluebells', 'Oranges and Lemons' and 'Sticky Glue'.

These children have just come in from playtime. They are getting ready to start lessons in their primary school in Woolwich, London.

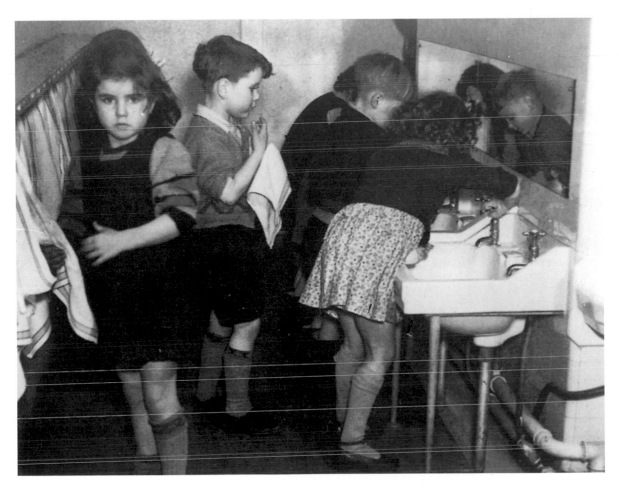

School 2

This photograph was taken inside a classroom in Mulberry Street Primary School, Hulme, Manchester. It was taken in 1956.

Janet Withersby remembers an important time in her primary school.

It seemed that the most important thing we were expected to do at my primary school was to pass the **11+ examination**. Children who passed the examination went to **grammar schools**; children who failed went to **secondary modern schools**. We practised special test papers every week in our last year in the juniors.

My 11+ day was 28 February 1955, which was a snowy day. The exam was held at a grammar school about three miles from home. We sat at desks in an enormous hall with a very high roof and were not allowed to speak. The examination lasted three hours.

In May, everyone in my primary school assembled in the hall to hear the list of exam passes read out. Everyone clapped the children who passed, and they were allowed to go home to tell their Mums. The children who failed just cried.

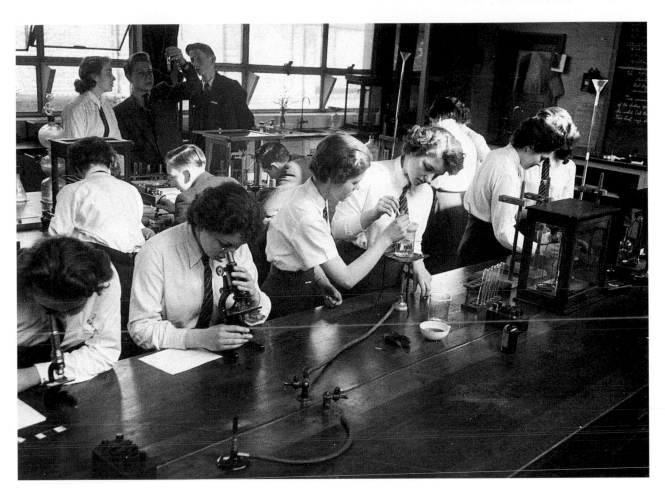

These girls are in a science class at the North Kensington Secondary School, London. They are doing experiments.

Derek Patterson describes the uniform he wore when he was 11.
The uniform was horrible. I had to wear a black blazer with black and white braiding all round the edge and a badge on the top pocket, a white shirt, black and white tie and grey socks. We had to wear short trousers until we were 14. If you weren't wearing your school cap when you went in through the gates, the **prefects** gave you lines. If you were caught three times, the Head caned you.

Margaret Simpkins remembers her school uniform.
When I went to grammar school I had a uniform for the first time. It was from the Co-op in Aberdare, and I was very proud of it. My blazer was green, edged in scarlet, and I had a green pinafore dress and a V-necked pullover. The pullover was the first 'shop' pullover I had ever had. Until then my mother had knitted all my jumpers. I also had a green **gabardine** macintosh which lasted all through school.

Work 1

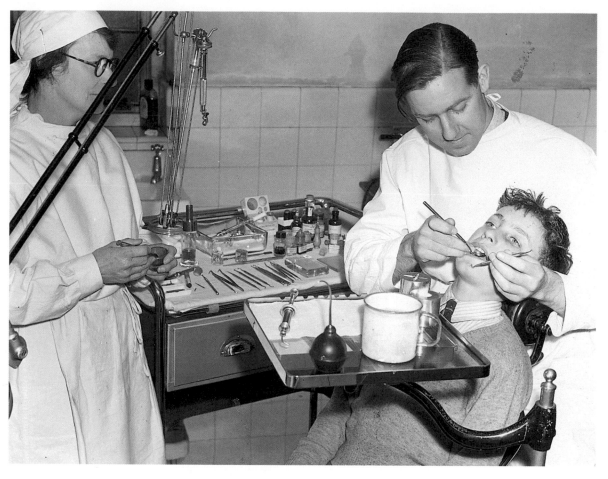

This school dentist worked for the National Health Service. He visited schools to check on pupils' teeth. This was a new idea in the 1950s.

Rosemary Dawson remembers a visit to the dentist.

Our dentist was called Mr Dare. He had his surgery in the back room of his house. I remember everything being shiny and very clean. While you were sitting in the shiny black dentist's chair you could see into his back garden. I hated visiting Mr Dare. There never seemed to be anything wrong with my teeth before I went, but he always found something to do to them. Most of all I hated the drill. It was at the end of a long, black jointed arm, and Mr Dare swung it out and round so that he could drill the exact tooth he had chosen. The drill ground away VERY slowly. There were no such things as injections, and if the drill hit a nerve in your tooth it hurt a lot. Sometimes I found it very difficult to keep still because he was hurting me so much. Mr Dare talked a lot while he worked. He was planning to **emigrate** to Australia with his family. I often wonder whether or not they went.

The fishermen have landed their catch at the port of Hull. The fish are being sorted before being packed in boxes with lots of ice.

Iain Williams remembers working on trawlers.

I had a good boss who owned three trawlers. He paid us a good wage when times were good and there were lots of fish, and when times were bad he still kept us on, though not on so much money, of course.

I could usually reckon on being at sea for about three weeks at a time, but a lot depended on whether we found the fish or not.

When we got to the North Sea fishing grounds we let out the **trawl**. This was an enormous net, shaped like a cone, which was towed behind the boat. It was easy to tell when the net was getting full because the trawler went slower and slower. When we judged it right, we hauled the net in and spilled all the fish onto the deck and into the hold. That was an exciting moment! We knew whether we were going to be paid well or not, and whether we should go home or stay out and do another trawl.

Work 2

These coal miners are being brought to the surface. They have just finished working their shift underground.

Bill Jenkins remembers working as a miner in south Wales.

We got really filthy dirty down the pit. I used to strip to the waist and, with a pick, dig out the very front edge of the coal seam. Sometimes I worked in a space no more than two feet high. I was always afraid that the roof of coal would come crashing in on me, or that I would break into a pocket of gas that would explode. Nothing like that ever happened to me, though it did to other miners in other pits. The team working beind me made the working space bigger and put up pit props to stop the whole thing collapsing. Of course, my work is done by machinery nowadays. In the 1950s it was very different. We had pit ponies to pull the tubs of coal to the shaft, and then to the surface. The ponies were well looked after, but spent about ten months of the year underground. It was marvellous to see how they frisked about when they were taken to the surface for their summer break in the fields.

This woman was a secretary. She typed letters. Her boss dictated a letter to her earlier and she wrote it down in shorthand on her pad.

Carole Feldman describes what she did when she left school in 1957.

In 1957 I took my 'O'-level exams. I passed five of them and decided to leave school. I didn't want to stay on and do more schoolwork. I wanted to be out earning my living with some money to spend.

My parents and I decided that the best thing for me would be to go to a secretarial college. The course lasted for six months. I learned typing and shorthand. Shorthand was interesting but hard to learn. Every sound had a special squiggle, and because words are made up of sounds, you could write down very quickly, in squiggles, what people said. So when your boss dictated a letter, you could get it down quickly and type it up later. When I left college, I could type 100 words a minute and take down 120 words a minute in shorthand. I got a job with a local firm of solicitors and stayed there until I married in 1964.

Spare Time 1

These are all comics which children read in the 1950s. Do they look anything like your comics?

Richard Dawson remembers the comics he read in the 1950s.

I think 'Swift' was the first real comic I had. I remember, though, thinking it was pretty babyish. Every story ended happily and all the children were so good! I was really relieved when I was allowed to move on to 'Eagle'. I really got involved in the adventures of Dan Dare and the Mekon, who had a huge green head and an enormous brain.

The comics I really enjoyed were 'Dandy' and 'Beano', where everyone had silly adventures. Desperate Dan always ended up eating an enormous cow pie.

My elder sister, Rosemary, had 'Girl', which was the girls' equivalent of 'Eagle', and 'School Friend'. I think they had mainly school stories in them, but I wasn't really interested. We were both supposed to read 'Children's Newspaper' which was very serious. Most of my friends' parents approved of 'Eagle', 'Girl' and 'Children's Newspaper'.

Michael Cawson remembers watching children's television in the 1950s.

I remember when we got our first television set. It was so exciting! The programme I remember well is 'Muffin the Mule'. Muffin was a metal puppet who was controlled by strings. Annette Mills used to talk to him and sing songs. Muffin would dance on top of the piano and his metal hooves would make a clip-clopping sound.

The big difference was that television programmes were only on at certain times. There was a series called 'Watch with Mother' which was on just after lunch. Each day there was a different programme. Most of them had puppets in them. I watched it while my Mum did the washing up. Then there were no programmes on television at all until about 5 o'clock. Then there were programmes for older children.

'Muffin the Mule' was a children's television programme, shown in the 1950s. Not many people had televisions at the time.

Spare time 2

Young people liked to go to dance halls. This photograph of young people dancing was taken in 1956.

Rosemary Dawson remembers how she learned to dance in the 1950s.
Sometime around 1957, my parents decided that I had to learn ballroom dancing. A local teacher was giving classes in the **Conservative Club** in the High Street, and this seemed too good a chance to miss. I didn't want to go by myself, so my school friend Gillian came along too. The classes were held once a week at a cost of three shillings and six pence a week.

The hall where the classes were held was dusty and had a wooden floor. The teacher set up her **gramophone** and all her records on the stage, and was most enthusiastic. Of course there were more girls than boys, and as girls and boys danced different steps, we girls ended up knowing the boys' parts for some of the dances! We learned the waltz, quickstep, tango and foxtrot, and something called the ballroom jive. We were only allowed to do this at the end, as a special treat.

THE NEW

Martin
LIGHTWEIGHT SPORTS CYCLES
by Hercules

WITH REYNOLDS "531" FRAME TUBES

Specially designed for the young club cyclist, modern lightweight construction, brilliantly finished . . . all that you expect from the makers of The Finest Bicycle Built To-day. Reynolds "531" Frame Tubes. 21 in. and 23 in. frame. $70\frac{1}{2}°$ head, $70\frac{1}{2}°$ seat angles. Maes handlebar bend. Racing rat-trap pedals, quill-type. Dunlop Sports Tyres. Finished Bright Blue or Sapphire Blue as standard, with unique distinctive Decorative Transfers.

PRICE **£13.12.6**
including Purchase Tax
(Speed Gears Extra)

Hercules *Martin*

Produced by the makers of
The Finest Bicycle Built To-day

THE HERCULES CYCLE & MOTOR CO. LTD., BIRMINGHAM, 6

Cycling was very popular in the 1950s, when there was less traffic on the roads than there is today. This is an advert for a Martin sports cycle.

Rosemary Dawson remembers learning to ride a bicycle.

My parents gave me a bicycle for passing the 11+ examination. I had found it hidden in the garden shed long before the results came out, so I guessed they were going to give it to me whether I passed or not.

Having a bicycle was one thing. Learning to ride it was quite another. Every evening my father took me out into the street. He held the saddle and ran behind while I pedalled and steered. As soon as he let go of the saddle, I fell off. Once I even steered into a lamppost. However, suddenly I was balancing on two wheels without falling off. I learned to pedal one handed while I put out my right or left arm to show which way I was turning, but I never managed to ride without my hands on the handlebar!

Holidays 1

These children are having fun on the beach. Richard Dawson is 'driving' and Rosemary is sitting at the back.

Richard Dawson remembers seaside holidays.

I can remember being very cross because my elder sister, Rosemary, was allowed to have a metal spade before I was. I know I was five years younger, but I really wasn't going to cut my toes off by accident! We both had metal buckets with pictures of Mickey Mouse on the outside.

We used to dig huge holes in the sand. Some of them were six feet deep and must have been quite dangerous.

We made sandcastles with complicated moats so that the tide, when it came in, would swirl round and not destroy the castle completely.

The worst part, of course, was leaving the beach. Our feet were washed in sea water, dried, and then we had to put our socks on. There was always some sand left between my toes, and my socks always got stuck when I tried to put them on. Walking back to the hotel in sticky socks and sandals always felt very odd.

This girl has fallen fast asleep in the train which is taking her home from her seaside holiday.

Susan Willoughby remembers going to Scotland on holiday.
About every three or four years, if we had enough money, we went to Scotland to visit my other grandparents. This was a great thrill because we went on the train. We usually travelled overnight because the fares were cheaper then. All the trains were pulled by steam engines, of course. I can remember having to change trains several times. It was especially exciting if we had to do this in the middle of the night. I will always remember the noise and smell of steam trains.

I remember once travelling in a carriage full of soldiers from one of the Scottish regiments wearing their colourful kilts.

One year my father decided he wanted to travel by road. He only had a motorbike and **sidecar**, so my mother, sister and brother went by train. Dad and I set off at 4 o'clock in the morning. It was a great adventure.

Holidays 2

Not everyone had holidays by the seaside. In these photographs the Dawson family are having a farm holiday in Cornwall.

Janet Withersby describes a different sort of holiday she had in 1955.

After the **Second World War** (1939–45) teachers in Liverpool and Cologne got together to find ways in which children from these two cities could become friends instead of enemies. My father was one of these teachers. When I was nine, my father found me a German friend called Annemarie. She was the niece of a German teacher. We wrote to each other in English because Annemarie had been learning English for two years. In 1955 I went to Germany to stay with Annemarie's family. They had food I had never seen: Swiss cheeses and cakes with real cream. I went to a birthday party in a house which had not been repaired since it had been damaged by bombs in the war. I was very shocked because in Liverpool there were no longer any signs of bomb damage. I had not expected to see any reminders of the war.

In the 1950s lots of people went to holiday camps. They slept in chalets, ate in large dining rooms and had organized fun.

Sue Mann remembers a summer holiday spent in a holiay camp.
We always went on holiday every year, even though I don't think my parents had a lot of money. We always went to the seaside, and stayed at either a **boarding house** or a holiday camp.

The whole family went on holiday together. This meant that my parents, grandparents, uncle, sister and I all travelled in one car! The family had bought the car together, and they were determined to use it together.

Whenever we went to a holiday camp, I was always entered in the fancy dress competition. I particularly remember one holiday camp when I was dressed up as an Hawaiian dancer. The family used yards and yards of crepe paper to make my costume – and I still didn't win!!

We spent a lot of time on the beach. My Dad always made the best sandcastles. We were always very proud when people came by and admired them.

Holidays 3

These two friends enjoyed eating candy-floss whilst on holiday in Blackpool.

Sally Jones remembers a long train journey from Hull to Helston, in Cornwall.

Every summer, I went with my parents to stay with the rest of our family in Cornwall. For days beforehand my mother packed our clothes in huge leather trunks and cases. Then the day came when we were to leave. Paragon Station in Hull was big, noisy and smelly. I used to stuff my fingers in my ears when the engines let off steam. Finally we were off, travelling in the Pullman coach, with porters to help with the luggage. We changed trains in London, and drove to Paddington in a taxi catching exciting glimpses of the city as we went. At last we were in our seats on the Cornish Riviera Express. We knew we were nearly there when we crossed the Tamar Bridge into Cornwall. Fourteen hours after leaving Hull we pulled up in Helston. My Uncle was always there to meet us. Now I could really look forward to a marvellous holiday.

Carole Feldman remembers a caravanning holiday when she was a child.

One summer my parents bought a touring caravan. The idea was that we would tour Devon and Cornwall, stopping off wherever we saw somewhere we liked. Dad had a **tow-bar** fixed on the car, and we set off.

One of the problems was that there were not many caravan sites. We had to ask friendly farmers if we could park in their fields. Most said 'Yes' and some let us use bathrooms and toilets in their farmhouses. Otherwise we had to manage as best we could.

The other problem was that it rained nearly all the time. The noise of rain drumming on the metal roof of a small caravan was deafening. My sister and I quarrelled a lot and got told off a lot. We had to wear our boots to go across the fields, and when we did get on a beach we were carrying our buckets and spades, wearing our sand shoes – and plastic macs!

Many families went on caravanning holidays. These people belong to a caravanners' club. They are meeting in Tatton Park, Knutsford.

Special Days 1

This family is having a good time at the Festival of Britain. It opened in London in 1951.

Elisabeth Bown remembers visiting the Festival of Britain.
We were all very excited when we were told that our school was going to take a party of children to the Festival of Britain. I think my name was first on the list!

The buildings I remember best were the Skylon, which was very tall, thin and cigar shaped, and the Dome of Discovery, which looked a bit like a mushroom. When it got dark all the buildings were lit up. It all looked so bright and new. We noticed this especially because everything else was so drab, and we had been used to darkness and not showing lights during the war.

The exhibit I remember best was one which made you feel you were inside an **atom**. You walked down a corridor on spongey rubber flooring as you were supposedly taken inside an atom. You could touch and feel the different parts. It was so different from anything I had seen before.

Susan Willoughby remembers the Queen visiting Rotherham in 1953.

After the Coronation, when the Queen was crowned, she toured Great Britain. She came to Rotherham in autumn 1953. I'm sure it was autumn because I remember endless rehearsals in my primary school playground on damp, chilly days. All the schools in the town had been given a place to stand on the royal route. Our teachers were anxious that we would all see the Queen, so we had to stand two deep with the smallest children in front. We then had to practise our flag-waving so that no one's view was blocked. I remember feeling silly and thinking it was a waste of time.

However, on the day of the Queen's visit, as we stood waiting to cheer and wave our flags, it all seemed worthwhile. The Queen passed by in a flash, of course, but even so we could tell our friends and family that we had seen her.

The coronation of Queen Elizabeth II was held on June 2 1953. Here the Queen and Prince Philip are driving through cheering crowds.

Special Days 2

These photographs were taken at Rosemary Dawson's birthday party on 19 May 1950, when she was 8-years-old.

Rosemary Dawson remembers her birthday party in 1950.

I had a party dress made from green shiny material. It had frills round the neck and middle and I hated it. I had to wear it, though! Over the dress I wore a fluffy white **angora** cardigan, which my mother had knitted. My grandfather gave me a **coral** necklace, and I wore that too. I wore white sandals and white socks.

My mother made marvellous food for my parties. We never had sandwiches – always bridge rolls with interesting fillings. There were meringues, which had been baked so slowly in the **Rayburn** that they were a wonderful pale coffee colour. My birthday cake was iced by the local baker and had pink rosebuds on it and icing sugar shells around the base.

It was lucky that my birthday was in May because the weather was usually good. My father organized the games and the prizes. He always made sure everyone won something.

Glossary

angora wool made from sheep's wool and angora rabbit hair.

atom the smallest particle that any piece of matter can be broken down into.

boarding house a place where people stayed while they went on holiday.

Conservative Club a club run for members of the Conservative Party, a political party.

Co-op the name of a shop. It is a short name for the Co-operative Society.

coral red or pink rock from under the sea.

dried milk powdered milk, mixed with water and fed to babies.

eleven plus (11+) examination: a test taken by children at 11-years-old that decided which secondary school children went to.

emigrate to leave your home country and settle in another country.

Festival of Britain an exhibition held in London, in 1951, designed to cheer people out of post-war gloom. A fantasy world of new buildings, furniture, sculpture etc. was created on the banks of the River Thames.

'G-Plan' a style of furniture popular in the 1950s.

gabardine heavy, hard wearing cloth used to make raincoats.

grammar school the school you went to if you passed the 11+ exam.

gramophone an old fashioned type of record player.

leatherette plastic material which was made to look like leather.

mangle a machine with two rollers. Clothes were passed through the rollers to squeeze water out of them, so that they dried quicker.

'O'-level exams short for 'Ordinary' level exams, which were taken by some pupils at 16.

prefects pupils who made sure that other pupils behaved themselves.

radiogram an old fashioned type of radio.

raffia type of straw used for making baskets.

ration book a book of coupons. Each coupon was exchanged for certain goods which were in short supply, like food, clothing and petrol. You were only allowed to have a certain amount of these goods during the war.

Rayburn a type of cooker.

secondary modern school the school you went to if you failed the 11+ exam.

Second World War war between the Axis Powers (Germany, Italy and Japan) and the Allies (Britain, Russia, France and the USA). It happened between 1939 and 1945.

shorthand a system of writing quickly in symbols, instead of words.

sidecar small car attached to the side of a motorbike, for extra passengers.

skewer a long, thin piece of metal used to hold meat together while it cooks. It can also be used for making holes in things.

starch a white powder, mixed with water and sprayed on material to make it stiff. It was used on shirt collars.

thong narrow strip of leather.

threepenny bit a coin worth three old pence (3d) – now worth 1p.

tow-bar a bar attached to a car, used for towing a caravan or a boat.

trawl to fish using a vary large net.

velour a soft fabric, like velvet.

whip and top a children's game. A wooden top was kept spinning by tapping it with a whip.

Index